Moxie and a Good Sense of Balance

Moxie and a Good Sense of Balance

Nancy Drew and the Power of the Teenage Girl

Lynne Byall Benson

HAMILTON BOOKS
Lanham • Boulder • New York • Toronto

The Rowman & Littlefield Publishing Group, Inc.
4501 Forbes Boulevard
Suite 200
Lanham, Maryland 20706
Hamilton Books Acquisitions Department (301) 459-3366

Unit A, Whitacre Mews, 26-34 Stannary Street,
London SE11 4AB, United Kingdom

British Library Cataloging in Publication Information Available
Library of Congress Control Number: 2018956217
ISBN: 978-0-7618-6811-8 (pbk. : alk. paper)
ISBN: 978-0-7618-6974-0 (Electronic)

I dedicate this, my first book, to my mother,
Mitzi Wolf Byall, who first introduced me to
Nancy Drew. Like Nancy, Mom had plenty of moxie!

Contents

Acknowledgments

This book would not have been possible without the support of my publisher, Rowman & Littlefield, and its imprint Hamilton Books. Their editors have been very patient in dealing with this book project written by a novice author, and I thank them most appreciatively.

In addition, I thank the chair of Women's, Gender, and Sexuality Studies at the University of Massachusetts Boston, Dr. Elora Chowdhury, who advocated for this project on my behalf, helping me obtain the subvention grant necessary for publication.

I also thank my fellow faculty members in the Women's, Gender, and Sexuality Studies Department for their unwavering support of this, my first foray into the publishing world.

Thanks, also, to my "Xian Sisters," Professors Chris Bobel, Carney Maley, Kristin Murphy, and Tara Parker, for their love and advice and for never asking me when my book will be finished.

Words cannot convey how much I have appreciated and enjoyed working with my copy editor, Deborah Justice. She loved this project as much as I did, and it showed in her expertise in helping make me a better writer. Thanks, DJ!

To my stepdaughters, Caetlin and Elisabeth Benson-Allott: I love you both so very much.

To my great "chum," Martha Fox: thank you for being a cheerleader on behalf of Nancy and me.

Finally, I thank my husband, John Benson. I love you, and you will always be my "Ned Nickerson."

Chapter One

Nancy's Timeless Appeal

Nancy Drew first saved the day on April 28, 1930, when she found the missing will, bested the interlopers, and set all to rights in *The Secret of the Old Clock*. But *I* first met her years later, in the 1960s, in the pages of my mother's copies of the original titles. As I approached adolescence I faithfully hoarded my babysitting money and allowance in eager anticipation of purchasing the next installment. During those confusing growing-up-years, I learned all too well that "being a teen is a challenge and a thrill, but it's exhausting." Reading Nancy Drew was a salve, because, I had found, she "offers girl readers something more than action-packed adventure: she gives them something original."[1] And perhaps it is because I steadily read Nancy Drew mysteries in my most impressionable years that she has remained with me as an adult.

And Nancy Drew endures today; since 1930, not a single Nancy Drew title has been out of print.[2] But why, when so many literary heroes have vanished from the cultural conversation altogether, has Nancy proven so resilient? Why has Nancy Drew continued to hold our attention over all these years? Maybe it's because she's so popular, good-looking, cheerful, well-loved, and *comfortable*; in short, Nancy seems to have so much of what many a reader would desire. And she certainly doesn't seem to suffer the anxieties typical of an ordinary teenage girl, granted an unusual level of autonomy. But I think her near-ageless appeal owes to more than this.

Nancy Drew is relevant to today's readers. She is, in short, a contemporary feminist role model for girls. Title by title, young heroine Nancy successfully solves complicated mysteries, often under the guise of assisting her father, famous criminal lawyer Carson Drew. In this she models confident, independent young womanhood. So, while Nancy not only possesses nearly every grace that would have been desired by an early twentieth-century girl reader, she also fully embodies qualities that would have been considered almost exclusively "masculine" in the 1930s and '40s, when the series' popularity was at its height: physical strength, resourcefulness, curiosity, and athleticism.

Undoubtedly, Nancy has morphed over the years as various ghostwriters have assumed the pen; but what interests us is the girl who first appeared in *The Secret of the Old Clock*, the young gumshoe who solved mysteries throughout the 1930s and '40s. This version of Nancy Drew seems to have managed to be both fully "feminine" while also exhibiting a remarkable independence that would have then typically been reserved for incorrigible boys—a moxie author Betsy Caprio calls Nancy's "Drew-ness."[3]

I don't mean to say that Nancy and the series are without flaw; the books are a product of their time and sometimes reflect the excesses or prejudices of the era. But at core Nancy Drew remains a timeless embodiment of confidence and agency, independent of changing cultural expectations for girls.

With the series' first installment in 1930, a new kind of literary exemplar was born. In an age when the virtuous young woman was praised for excelling in the home arts and appealing to marriageable young men, Nancy Drew managed to fully live both in *and outside of* what was considered her appropriate, gendered sphere. Qualities that read as novel in the 1930s and '40s are explicitly aspirational to today's young girl readers. And so it is the marriage of typically and atypically feminine qualities so easily assumed by Nancy that I think make her a role model for today's young women.

In my work, I reexamine images of protofeminism, but it wasn't until fairly recently that I began to explore in this light why Nancy holds such an attraction for me. As I am a scholar by profession, I naturally spent a great deal of time methodically considering the question. First, I reread my stash of old Nancy Drew books; in so doing, I began to realize that it was the earlier Nancy of the first decades of her popularity that held greater appeal for me than did the character's later iterations. I then dove into the literary critique. Before long Betsy Caprio became my articulate and perceptive guide in this process, through her most excellent book, *The Mystery of Nancy Drew: Girl Sleuth on the Couch.*

My systematic reexamination of each Nancy Drew title also considered the illustrations included in the first editions of the series. Each cover and frontispiece shows Nancy elegantly clad in the dress of the era—which makes her look so much more adult than the typical sixteen-year-old girl we know today. On most of the covers, Nancy is hiding from the book's villains, a promise of suspense drawing us in: *She could be discovered at any minute!* And we never have to turn so very many pages before we are met by Nancy's freedom, poise, and capacity to do it all. In fact, we are first introduced to Nancy thus:

> Nancy finished her breakfast and then went to the kitchen to consult with Hannah, the maid, concerning the work of the day. Although only sixteen, Nancy was unusually capable, and under her skillful direction everything ran smoothly in the Drew household.
>
> On the death of her mother six years before, she had taken over the entire management of the establishment. The Drews employed one servant, Hannah Gruen, an elderly maid of all work who had been with them for many years.
>
> The responsibility of the household might have weighed heavily upon Nancy, but she was the type of girl who is capable of accomplishing a great many things in a comparatively short length of time. She enjoyed sports of all kinds, and she found time for clubs and parties. In school Nancy had been very popular, and she boasted many friends. People declared that she had a way of taking life very seriously without impressing one as being the least bit serious herself.[4]

Poised, decisive, discerning, resourceful, efficient, athletic, sociable, popular, well-loved . . . What young girl *wouldn't* want to be like Nancy? The Nancy of those earliest books glows with the best qualities most appreciated in good girls of the 1930s; and Nancy's independence, athleticism, and strength come off the page just as favorably, even if they might better describe an esteemed *boy* of that age. In any case, this fine amalgam of qualities definitely appealed to my younger self, searching as I was for my first role model outside of the female members of my family—as would any adolescent female beginning her normal development toward adulthood, effecting a slow separation from family of origin.

For all their original popularity, the Nancy Drew books could well have faded into memory, like most books do. But woven into Nancy Drew's cloth was something tough and timeless, something that manages to be fresh and relevant even to young readers today. This means that, as Nancy's original fans outgrew the series, newer readers found her, found her *relevant*, and embraced her. Instead of discarding the mores of 1930s-era heroines as hopelessly old-fashioned, this second generation of Nancy readership was born. During feminism's second wave, in the 1970s, Western women began consciously embracing the same stereotypically male traits that Nancy had seamlessly worn for decades. It is this confident straddling of gender boundaries, I think, that rounds out her appeal for today's girl readers, who are just as likely to be asked to put away their soccer cleats as their dolls and who are just as likely to dream about being president as they are being a princess.

In the following pages we explore the cultural, professional, and personal milieus in which Nancy Drew was brought to life. We follow her progression from plucky girl sleuth to chipper debutante to sexy jet-setter. We see that as time passed and American culture shifted, so did Nancy, her presence on the page altering subtly, and sometimes jarringly, with each new ghostwriter holding the pen. But in the end, it was the first Nancy—spirited, curious, energetic, able, independent—who captured readers' hearts and to whose mold the series eventually returned. And it is Nancy's DNA from which some of today's most memorable fictional icons are formed.

Almost ninety years and countless adventures later, Nancy Drew has as much to teach us today as she did when she first delighted. For, invaluable to any successful caper, as any bright, curious girl knows, are "moxie and a good sense of balance . . . when crawling on a roof."[5]

NOTES

1. Carole Kismaric and Marvin Heiferman, *The Mysterious Case of Nancy Drew and the Hardy Boys* (New York: Simon & Schuster, 1998). A portion of this book's title, *Moxie and Good Sense of Balance*, is borrowed from Jennifer Worick, *Nancy Drew's Guide to Life* (Philadelphia: Running Press, 2001). The book's epigraph is quoted from Carole Kismaric and Marvin Heiferman, *The Mysterious Case of Nancy Drew and the Hardy Boys* (New York: Simon & Schuster, 1998).

2. Jessica Harrison, "Girl Sleuth: Timeless Nancy Drew Series Celebrates 80 Years of Popularity," *Deseret News*, May 17, 2010, https://www.deseretnews.com/article/700032881/Girl-sleuth-Timeless-Nancy-Drew-series-celebrates-80-years-of-popularity.html.

3. Betsy Caprio, *The Mystery of Nancy Drew: Girl Sleuth on the Couch* (Trabuco Canyon, CA: Source Books, 1992), 22.

4. Originally published as Carolyn Keene, *The Secret of the Old Clock* (New York: Grosset & Dunlop, 1930). I draw the above quotation from a later edition, published as Carolyn Keen, *The Secret of the Old Clock*, facsimile edition (Bedford, MA: Applewood Books, 1991), 12–13. Any quotations hereafter from this title are from the 1991 facsimile edition.

5. Worick, *Nancy Drew's Guide to Life*, 12.

Chapter Two

The Stratemeyer Syndicate and the Modern Woman

On October 4, 1862, Edward Stratemeyer was born to German immigrants Henry and Anna Stratemeyer. Edward grew up with his six older siblings in Elizabeth, New Jersey, and worked in his father's successful tobacco store, where he developed a head for business and a spirit for entrepreneurship.[1] All of the Stratemeyer children were artistically accomplished, but it was Edward who always knew he would become a writer. "I think I must have been about six years old when I attempted to write my first story," he recalled later in life.[2] As a boy, Edward counted among his possessions a toy printing press and would go about his neighborhood publishing articles and interviews of the locals and his family.

He was valedictorian of his high school class, and, although he did not attend college, he received further schooling in rhetoric, composition, and literature.[3] Working at what was now his brother's tobacco shop, Edward continued to write, managing to publish in various children's magazines. As he honed his craft and found success as a writer, he could eventually afford to move from his parents' home to nearby Newark, where he soon owned and operated a stationery store.

In 1889 he married Magdelena Van Camp. Lenna, as she was known, encouraged her husband's writing, frequently editing and helping him publish his work, despite her frequent poor health.[4] With his wife's able assistance—and though they were simultaneously raising their two daughters, Harriet and Edna—Edward managed to produce an impressive forty-two dime novels between 1892 and 1893.[5]

In these early years, Edward Stratemeyer modeled his writing on the self-reliant characters found in the rags-to-riches tales spun by his literary hero, Horatio Alger. But in 1899, Edward broke from his custom in publishing the first installment of *The Rover Boys*, what would become among the most successful of boys' and girls' series books. In this series, rather than climbing from the lower ranks of society up the ladder of success in Alger-esque style, brothers Tom, Dick, and Sam Rover were solidly middle class. Edward positioned them enviably: While class privilege meant the boys were never burdened with money worries; they still managed to enjoy considerable freedom, as their mother was dead, their father was "exploring in Africa," and the brothers and been shipped off to boarding school, where there was apparently no adult supervision and they were free to head off on their own adventures. "A face at the window, a missing suitcase, or the overheard conversation . . . were sufficient to send the Rovers off on stirring trips that lasted for 52,000 words."[6]

Edward was evidently quite surprised by the success of the Rover Boys series, which he'd penned under the pseudonym "Arthur M. Winfield." "Twelve years ago the line was started with the publication of the first three stories," he modestly wrote in the forward of the fifteenth Rover Boys mystery, "never did I anticipate the tremendously enthusiastic welcome . . . the steady sales, ever increasing."[7]

By 1905 Edward had perfected a strategy that ensured his series were among the most successful of the genre. His formula for churning out entertaining novels was, rather than doing all the writing himself, to develop the plot outlines and characters and then hire other writers to flesh out the stories. He would then sell the completed works to publishers, retaining the rights for himself. In this manner Edward managed to publish successfully at a startling rate. His good friend Howard Garis used the same formula to publish the Tom Swift series under the name "Victor Appleton" and the Baseball Joe series under the name "Lester Chadwick." At this same time, Edward was introducing several series aimed at girls, beginning with the Bobbsey Twins (as "Laura Lee Hope") and the Ruth Fielding series (as "Alice B. Emerson").

Edward expanded his stable of writers, and between 1910 and 1930 the group averaged over thirty new titles per year; this was in addition to the installations to his thirty-one different series and the four books he wrote annually himself. His books became all the rage, and according to a 1926 survey, "Ninety-eight percent of kids . . . name[d] a Stratemeyer character as their favorite."[8] By 1940 the Stratemeyer Syndicate, as it had become known, created approximately half of all of the most popular juvenile series books in the United States.[9]

Edward carefully formulated the precise rules by which each author was to write a series book: "The recipe called for twenty-five chapters per book, each ending with a cliff-hanging episode. There was to be no touching or kissing and no upsetting violence; in fact no character could be knocked unconscious more than once per book, no matter how convenient a plot device. Action had to be intense enough to require exclamation marks galore."[10] With all the efficiency of a Ford assembly line, a Stratemeyer book took forty days to produce, from concept to release. And the sales didn't disappoint either.

At that time in the publishing world at large, girls' series books were gradually gaining prevalence, often surpassing the boys' series in popularity; this was especially true of those girls' series created by the Stratemeyer Syndicate, whose heroines were often independent, self-sufficient, and physically attractive. Consider, for example, the Moving Picture Girls (1914–1916), who created lives for themselves in Hollywood when their father lost his voice and subsequently found fame as a silent movie actor.[11] Or the Outdoor Girls, whose Girl Scout troop waged intercamp warfare with the Boy Scouts, soundly besting them in various outdoorsy feats. Or Ruth Fielding, who emerged as a role model for the 1920s: an attractive, entrepreneurial young woman who owned an independent film studio, "writing scripts, producing movies, and starring in them—juggling a successful Hollywood career with the demands of everyday life."[12] By 1920, 30 percent of all Stratemeyer Syndicate sales were girls' series books.[13]

Adolescent influence on American culture had certainly been making itself felt in the publishing industry. In 1929, more than thirty-one million books were marketed to youth and children—an increase of almost three times the number of titles targeting that demographic published the previous decade.[14] Edward Stratemeyer had positioned himself well to profit. But a 1926 survey by the American Library Association showed that, though he may have won over countless youthful readers, their elders remained somewhat more skeptical. Edward Stratemeyer, the ALA charged, was responsible for most of the "formulaic, sometimes sensationalistic series books . . . that librarians vilified as subliterate." In fact, many librarians "found that series fiction [was] destructive to young people's mental and physical well-being."[15] In addition to the ALA's consensus that series fiction offered little to no cultural value, the organization felt children were being negatively affected by "the intrusion of commercial values into the culture of childhood."[16] But young readers managed to ignore these disapproving warnings and buoyed the Stratemeyer Syndicate's success. "As oil had its Rockefeller," *Fortune Magazine* wrote, "literature had its Stratemeyer."[17]

And so when the humming Stratemeyer Syndicate produced a literary novelty, the world took notice.

"Nancy Drew," according to author Amy Boesky, "with her titian blonde hair and sporty roadster, is often seen . . . as the apotheosis of modernity—she is quick-thinking, partial to new gadgets, ever on the move."[18] To best understand Nancy Drew's modernity, we must understand the culture in which she was created.

In the years following World War I, industrialization and urbanization had been underway for several decades and were fast changing the norms of American culture beyond recognition, both at home and at work. And from the postwar prosperity was arising a new phenomenon: youth culture.

Female youth culture of the1920s was frequently represented by the so-called "flapper"—an independent young woman not bound by traditional social conventions. The flapper became an ideal of the modern young woman of the day: she considered herself equal to men and as such shed certain traditional conventions, planting a stylishly shod foot firmly in the public space, reflecting the freedom and public voice many women were finally claiming. Responding to this perceived equality, young women increasingly engaged in behaviors previously restricted to men, such as public drinking and smoking, and sexual experimentation. The availability of the automobile represented new opportunities for both young women and men to engage in these activities, independent of adult chaperonage.

The Jazz Age filled dance halls with young couples whose moves to this exciting, modern music grew increasingly sexually suggestive, "tribal rhythms ratcheting up heart-stopping levels of intensity."[19] Meanwhile, young women were celebrating their newly won suffrage by emancipating themselves of the previous era's overly heavy garments and restrictive corsets: the new, chic, *short* dresses they donned swung more loosely from the body and showed much more bare skin. "Fashion," says historian Jon Savage, "went hand-in-hand with changing morality. The increased sexual assertion of young women . . . was reinforced by the slow spread of short haircuts . . . and the slow rise of the skirt to just below the knee."[20]

With increased urbanization and clustered community came the ubiquity of cultural fads. And "by 1920, 37 percent of fourteen- to seventeen-year-olds enrolled in secondary school, strengthening peer culture."[21] High schools, therefore, not only segregated adolescents but also provided an environment in which societal trends were reinforced.

In 1904 psychologist G. Stanley Hall had published a two-volume study first identifying *adolescence*—that period between the ages of fourteen to twenty-four—as a specific phase of development in a person's life. However, according to scholar of youth culture Amy Boesky, Hall "pathologized adolescence, defining it as a period of crisis and debilitation requiring careful supervision and management."[22] Adolescents, Hall believed, were only partially evolved, devoid of the tools to manage their own erratic, undisciplined behavior; discipline and supervision were crucial if adolescents were to emerge as civilized adults—and by this he meant developing "health and hygiene, superabundant energy, a willingness to be taxed or 'stretched,' sympathy, love of nature, sublimation, activity, and loyalty or fidelity, both to self and community."[23]

But within little more than a decade, Hall performed an apparent about-face, actually endorsing the flapper; he now associated her with normative female adolescent development in the modern age and became an advocate for young women's freedom. In a 1922 *Atlantic Monthly* article, "The Flapper Americana Novissima," Hall posited that women's participation in World War I had helped liberalize young women's behavior, contributing "to her emancipation from the chaperon, and it became good patriotic form to address, give flaglets, badges, and dainties to young men in the street, and perhaps, strike up an acquaintance with them if they were in uniform. . . . Her manners have grown a bit free-and-easy, and every vestige of certain old restraint have gone."[24] However cautionary Hall may once have been in that original 1904 study pathologizing certain aspects of adolescence, by the Roaring Twenties he was pointing out the value of consumer goods, and certain behaviors, to female adolescent development.

Hall now recognized that the conduct of young women as consumers was a necessary part of the passage to adulthood. This healthy consumerism included purchasing certain products that had only recently been relegated to mainstream use. It meant wearing cosmetics, which had previously been considered the paint of prostitutes. It meant wearing the latest fashions. It meant learning the latest dance steps. It meant going out to "movies," that exciting, newest advance in entertainment. And in 1927, a mere three years before the world first met Nancy Drew, one silent film caused an uproar and overnight turned its star into the original "It" girl and patron saint of aspiring flappers everywhere.

Based on a short story by popular author Elinor Glyn, the film *It* tells the story of a sexually liberated shop girl who pursues romance with her boss. Actress Clara Bow's portrayal of the ideal flapper catapulted her career to the stratosphere and continued to normalize young women's pursuit of sexual freedom. Glyn's use of the word *it* became synonymous with sex appeal, "a symbol for the most desirable thing the gods could give . . . a tremendous attraction to the opposite sex."[25] The cultural impact was immediate and lasting. After the film's release, high school students voted which of their classmates had "It." And even today headlines breathlessly, regularly, christen Hollywood's newest "It" girl.

Having "It," "coupled with the flapper's self-confidence, marked a new kind of social ritual for young women that enabled them to successfully pass through their adolescence."[26] G. Stanley Hall's endorsement of the flapper was echoed by other prominent members of society, including popular author F. Scott Fitzgerald and his wife, Zelda, often considered the first American flapper. In 1920 Fitzgerald published his first collection of short stories, *Flappers and Philosophers*, thrusting him and Zelda into the public eye. American youth culture of that age was perfectly personified by *his* literary treatment of Jazz Age culture and *her* striking looks and party-girl spirit. In Zelda's 1922 essay "Eulogy on the Flapper," she "firmly stated that the freedoms for which the 'first Flappers' like her had fought . . . to bob her hair, . . . to put on 'a great deal of audacity and rouge' . . . and to flirt . . . had become accepted as the standard of the first mass female adolescent generation."[27]

The modern American woman had been born.

NOTES

1. Young Stratemeyer "learned the basics of commerce and, especially, entrepreneurship," according to Melanie Rehak, *Girl Sleuth: Nancy Drew and the Women Who Created Her* (Orlando: Harcourt, 2005), 6.

2. Ibid.

3. Ibid., 7.

4. Ibid., 9.

5. Ibid., 18.

6. Ibid., 22.

7. Carol Billman, *The Secret of the Stratemeyer Syndicate: Nancy Drew, the Hardy Boys, and the Million Dollar Fiction Factory* (New York: The Ungar Publishing Company, 1986), 3.

8. Caprio, *Mystery of Nancy Drew*, 22.

9. Ibid., 15.

10. Ibid.

11. Ibid., 16.

12. Ibid.

13. Kismaric and Heiferman, *The Mysterious Case of Nancy Drew*.

14. Leonard S. Marcus, *Minders of Make-Believe: Idealists, Entrepreneurs, and the Shaping of American Children's Literature* (New York: Houghton Mifflin Co., 2008), 104.

15. Ibid., 105.

16. Ibid., 106.

17. As quoted in ibid.

18. Amy Boesky, "Solving the Crime of Modernity: Nancy Drew in 1930," Studies in the Novel, *The Young Adult Novel* 42, nos. 1–2 (Spring and Summer 2010), 185–201.

19. Jon Savage, *Teenage: The Prehistory of Youth Culture, 1875–1945* (New York: Penguin Books, 2007), 173.

20. Ibid., 202.

21. Boesky, "Solving the Crime of Modernity," 186.

22. Ibid.

23. Ibid., 188.

24. As quoted in Savage, *Teenage*, 202.

25. Mark Sullivan, *Our Times: The United States, 1900–1925*, vol. 6, The Twenties (New York: Charles Scribner's Sons, 1935), 401–402.

26. Savage, *Teenage*, 202.

27. Ibid., 200.

Chapter Three

Authoring an Icon

A *dame*, Merriam-Webster tells us, is "a woman of rank, station, or authority," "the mistress of a household," or "a female member of an order of knighthood."[1] But the colloquial dame of the first decades of the twentieth century was something altogether more daring: a spirited woman, smart and resourceful, magnetic and commanding—the kind of woman more and more women were emulating. The Stratemeyer Syndicate's peppy, competent heroines were selling books like gangbusters, so by 1926 Edward began looking for more writers to create material to feed his publishing machine.

When he placed an ad in *Editor* magazine, budding writer Mildred Augustine answered from Clinton, Iowa. "I have sold a number of articles, feature stories and fiction," she wrote Edward, "and . . . about six hundred printed inches of newspaper material each week for the last year."[2] Suitably impressed with her qualifications, Stratemeyer set up a meeting with Mildred in New York City, which by all accounts went well. So when Mildred returned to Iowa to complete her master's degree, Edward stayed in touch.

It wasn't long before he asked Mildred to work on the Ruth Fielding series. She agreed to pen the upcoming title, *Ruth Fielding and Her Great Scenario*. Author Melanie Rehak points out that at that time the Ruth Fielding series was the most successful of the syndicate's girls' series, for "Ruth had been established as a go-getter and had made the shift from solving tame crimes at her boarding school to cracking Hollywood cases, even as she kept up a back-breaking workload in the movie industry."[3] What wasn't to love? "Ruth Fielding . . . is nothing if not a thoroughly modern girl."[4]

It wouldn't be a stretch to say that Ruth Fielding wasn't just modern—she was outright ahead of her time. Struggling with the dilemma of combining her career with an impending marriage put Ruth decades ahead of the curve of real-life early twentieth-century America, where remaining single had become "a pitiable social faux pas."[5] And Ruth's fiancé, Tom Cameron, was similarly forward-thinking, showing remarkable support for her choices. "Ruth," he vowed, "I'll never say a word about your career."[6] This was an idealistic response to a very real social quandary: whether or not Mildred Augustine herself struggled with the question we cannot say, but she chose to broach and resolve the issue in her portrayal of Ruth Fielding. Mildred herself was engaged to be married and "was determined to learn the business of book writing before she settled down, and to have something of her own even after she married."[7]

Ultimately, Mildred's authorial choices paid off, and Edward Stratemeyer was quite satisfied with her depiction of Ruth Fielding "as a forward-thinking, multitalented girl who always kept her head in an emergency and was by far the most well-informed person, male or female, in any situation."[8] In Ruth Fielding we see early sketches of the eminently capable Nancy Drew.

By 1927 the detective mystery had emerged as a popular genre for adults, and Edward thought it would be a good idea to introduce a version for his adolescent audience. In response, the highly successful Hardy Boys series was developed, written by Leslie McFarlane, a former reporter, who used the pen name "Franklin W. Dixon." The Hardy Boys series did well from the get-go, eventually publishing almost 120,000 mysteries, and by 1928 Stratemeyer felt the time was right to develop a female counterpart. In May of that year newly married Mildred Wirt, née Augustine, wrote Edward that she had relocated to Cleveland, where her husband worked for the Associated Press. She made it clear that though she was married she intended to continue working as a writer. And preferably for the Stratemeyer Syndicate.

Meanwhile, Edward and his publisher, Grossett & Dunlap, were moving forward with a new mystery series for girls, which would feature a teenage heroine. His sample plot outline for *The Secret of the Old Clock*, which involved a missing will, elicited an enthusiastic response from his publishers, who suggested a name change for the main character, whom he had been calling "Stella Strong." Edward adopted their suggestion and then wrote Mildred Wirt to ask if she might be interested in writing the first three books of the series under the pseudonym "Carolyn Keene." *The Secret of the Old Clock*, *The Hidden Staircase*, and *The Bungalow Mystery*, he told her, would feature sixteen-year-old amateur sleuth Nancy Drew.

A deal was struck, and by October 1, 1929, the contract was signed: the books "were to sell for fifty cents each, returning a royalty of two cents per copy for the Syndicate. Mildred would be paid $125 for each manuscript and, as usual, would sign away her rights to the stories and characters as soon as she handed in the manuscripts."[9] And so it was that Mildred Wirt became the first "Carolyn Keene," a pseudonym inextricable from Nancy Drew fame.

With the first installment's publication in 1930, Wirt introduced the world to sixteen-year-old Nancy Drew, her father (famed criminal lawyer Carson Drew), the fictional town of River Heights, and Nancy's beloved car, a "bright blue roadster, low slung, and smart. . . . The driver, a pretty girl . . . attractive in a frock which either by accident or design exactly matched the blue of the automobile."[10] Nancy Drew is attractive in both person and personality, enjoys an independent, privileged lifestyle predicated on her father's professional success, and is unencumbered by the typical adolescent parental clashes—her father busy at work and her mother having died when Nancy was three, making her "the sole wise mistress of her charming upper-class household." What's more, "the sixteen-year-old sleuth did not attend school and had no worries about money, career, or marriage."[11]

The Drew household resided "in a comfortable, tree-shaded Colonial brick home with a circular drive—the affluent American version of fairyland."[12] Carson Drew had raised his daughter almost as a peer, consulting her on his cases; indeed, that is how Nancy would become involved in many of the mysteries she invariably solved. On other occasions, the mysteries would be brought to her attention by friends asking for her help—help finding the missing will, as in *The Secret of the Old Clock*; help recovering the stolen jewels, as in *The Secret at Lilac Inn*; or help rescuing the kidnapped heiress, as in *The Bungalow Mystery*. Whatever had gone missing—wills, jewels, or people—Nancy always prevailed. By the final page of each volume, all was rightfully restored and the girl detective had another notch in her magnifying glass.

The series was a huge success. Prior to its publication, "earlier series for girls [had] focused on girls in groups. . . . By the time Nancy came along, the public was ready for a strong female who performed in a decidedly masculine way in a truly masculine profession yet managed to exemplify all the female virtues."[13] And Nancy Drew fit the bill. She was intelligent, attractive, sociable, self-sufficient, privileged, and remarkably free-ranging for a girl of only sixteen. Unduly constrained by parental constraints—her mother having died years ago and her father never choosing to remarry and not appearing to date—Nancy enjoyed a great deal of latitude while still benefitting from the unoppressive and accommodating attention of her single parent.

In fact, Carson Drew was something of an ideal parent. Writer and therapist Betsy Caprio describes him as "affirming, devoted affectionate, concerned, and generous. Is Nancy's roadster disabled while she's on a case? Her father is at hand with a replacement. . . . He not only looks distinguished but also is brilliant, successful, athletic, and humorous. Like his daughter, he has a pair of twinkling blue eyes."[14]

Since Mrs. Drew's death years ago, "[Nancy] and her dad have been a team—in his words, 'Drew & Drew.' Carson involves Nancy in his cases, appreciates her insights, and is proud of her record as a detective. . . . When she is not taken seriously by police officials or other authority figures, she identifies herself as Carson Drew's daughter, and opposition melts away."[15] A typical example of this deferential treatment is shown in *The Bungalow Mystery*, in which Nancy is attempting to recover the stolen Crandell jewels:

> The captain hesitated as he remembered he had not heard Nancy's name.
>
> "Drew," she replied automatically.
>
> "Drew!" Captain Dudley repeated in astonishment. "You're not related to Carson Drew, by chance?"

> "He is my father."
> "Jove! I know him well!"
> He turned to the crowd with decision.
> "Gentlemen, I can vouch for this girl. Her father is a famous criminal lawyer in River Heights."[16]

Carson Drew takes Nancy seriously and treats her like an adult, notwithstanding that in the early mysteries she was written to be but sixteen years of age. "It was his secret boast that he had taught her how to think for herself and to think logically."[17]

We see reflected in the Nancy Drew titles of the 1930s a freedom of movement and purchasing power newly won by the era's young women: Nancy and her friends lunch, shop, and socialize. "Arm in arm," Carolyn Keene writes of one evening out, "the two girls hurried up the path to the inn. . . . They were promptly escorted to a secluded nook which permitted an excellent view of the grounds." Some time later, on a shopping spree, Nancy's friend Helen bemoans, "I'm invited to a week-end party and I simply haven't a thing to wear."[18] Like an increasing number of American teens, Nancy and chums enjoyed every modern concession appropriate to their class privilege.

Within this context, Nancy Drew embodied psychologist G. Stanley Hall's modern adolescent girl—albeit one less overtly sexualized than the full-fledged flapper formed in Clara Bow and Zelda Fitzgerald's image. Nancy was a balance of virtues: She was reliable and disciplined, exuding responsibility and can-do. She embodied health and vigor, cultivated an active social life, and enjoyed both a stable, caring home life and loving, loyal friendships. She was, in a word, the very model of a civilized, modern adolescent. Nowhere did she evidence Hall's dreaded "pathology" of adolescence, instead demonstrating an "inherent . . . sense of right and wrong."[19] She was the stalwart and reliable teen Hall favored who never sacrificed the agency, independence, and verve so favored by the flapper. She was a *dame*.

Though Nancy came to print after the height of the age of the flapper, she still spoke to her female readership. And her popularity did not falter even as the times grew increasingly tumultuous. On October 29, 1929—a mere two weeks after Mildred Wirt and Edward Stratemeyer first reached their agreement on developing the Nancy Drew mysteries—the stock market crashed, sending the American economy into a tailspin. Over a thousand banks would fail in the aftermath. By 1930, "the average income of the American family had sunk to $1,428," with only "25.4 percent of women work[ing] outside the home."[20] The wealthy Stratemeyer family and their ilk, however, were seemingly unaffected by the country's economic hardships, and Nancy Drew was drawn in their image.

Perhaps this explains why the series remained popular throughout the Great Depression, offering, as Amy Boesky posits, "an escape from the harsh realities of the Depression, a collective fantasy of middle-class empowerment, as . . . Nancy Drew feature[d] [an] idealized adolescent protagonist with phenomenal yet recognizable skills; [she] was a competent problem solver able to set a disordered world right again."[21]

Through Nancy her readership could still enjoy the finer things. When we first meet her, she is "dressed to the nines in smart tweed suits, cloche hats, and fancy dresses—'including a party frock that matched her eyes,'" notes literary critic Melanie Rehak. This new literary heroine had been carefully calibrated to win over the broadest spectrum of readers—aspirational but not elitist: "Pretty enough to be exceptional but not so pretty that she would alienate readers, she was also in possession of not only admirable intellect, but a shiny blue roadster."[22]

But Nancy likewise reassured a readership right on the cusp of adulthood, not immune to the precariousness wrought by the Great Depression. "River Heights, Nancy's attractive Midwestern town, was hermetically sealed off from unemployment and hard times that were crashing like tidal waves over the country." Reading about Nancy's charmed life was escapism from the grim economics of the Depression, reminding "everyone that the good old days, the days of frills and festivities, of tea parties and a maid to do the cooking, were not so far gone."[23]

In addition to reflecting Edward Stratemeyer's upper-middle-class status, Nancy was infused with some of ghostwriter Mildred Wirt's own wit and independence. The novels portrayed self-reliant young woman who was serially embroiled in exciting escapades—and who always acquitted herself well. Whether solving a haunting or recovering heirloom jewels, with each new plot outline Mildred wrote, Nancy Drew retained a defining resourcefulness and gumption. But her world also began to expand as Mildred contextualized her socially.

It is in the third book of the series, *The Bungalow Mystery*, that readers first meet the two female characters who would reappear in numerous subsequent mysteries—Nancy's chums: her cousin, the hyper-feminine Bess Marvin, and Bess's tomboyishly behaving and tomboyishly named cousin, George Fayne. According to Rehak, the introduction of these two characters, seemingly at the opposite ends of the scale of femininity for the times, gave fans of all sorts the opportunity to comfortably identify with the series. For, "if you were not as perfect as Nancy, surely you were at least a interesting enough to be like—and thus be—one of the closest chums of the queen bee."[24]

Author and literary critic Bobbie Ann Mason underscores Bess and George's relatability. "Nancy sleuths virtually unaided," she points out; the two chums "spend most of their time hanging around . . . going shopping or drinking tea, while Nancy figures and figures. They are recognizable only by their loyalty and as mirrors of Nancy's two halves, demonstrating the extreme options open to females—tomboy and fluffhead."[25]

The experiment with widening Nancy's social circle having been well received, Nancy was now to be given a beau. Our first glimpse of Ned Nickerson is when he "rescues Nancy, George, and Bess from a fender bender they've gotten into on the way home from investigating a mysterious fire."[26] Like Bess and George, Ned becomes a regular in the series, and he is a likable enough addition to Nancy's universe. Enrolled at nearby Emerson College, he is always willing to escort Nancy to country club dances and social engagements. But his squiring never extends to playing bodyguard: while he's always game to accompany her on her sleuthing outings, he very rarely rescues her from any of the numerous tight spots she finds herself in. Our girl is nothing if not self-sufficient.

Though Nancy seems fond of Ned, however, "she is not gaga about him."[27] "On one occasion," Caprio points out, "Ned's overture about their [married] future is countered by Nancy with, 'Ned, someday I'll promise to listen.' She is just not ready."[28]

And so Nancy enjoys all the perks of a steady boyfriend (romance, a date to all of her parties) without any of the headache (unwanted sexual tension and pressure). Bobbie Ann Mason further points out that "Nancy has Ned under her thumb, and she must keep him there if she is to protect her purity. . . . The

Nancy Drew books cleverly (and no doubt unintentionally) conceal sexual fascination, especially since Nancy is frequently embarrassed by Ned's attentions. . . . Every time Ned gets Nancy alone, a mystery intervenes."[29]

Just as Nancy's social sphere broadens, so does her her landscape, and in the series' fifth installment, *The Secret of Shadow Ranch*, Nancy and friends are removed from the familiar confines of River Heights out West to a ranch. There the three girls are under the chaperonage of Bess and George's Aunt Nell, who is much occupied preparing the homestead for sale. The three friends are left to fill their time with horseback riding and any number of other outdoor activities. But when venturing beyond the safety of the property, Aunt Nell insists they carry a gun—one of the few times the series arms its girl hero. Assumed to be the most competent and responsible in the group, Nancy holsters the gun herself. And thank goodness, because she saves the day, expertly shooting an attacking lynx. She further demonstrates her übercompetence when a severe storm sweeps in and a resulting flash flood imperils Bess and her mount. Predictably, Nancy is the best horsewoman in the group, handily coming to their aid. When Bess gasps that Nancy has saved her life, our heroine demurs: "All I did was grab hold of the bridle."[30]

And if multiple near-death experiences, acts of God, and close calls with ferocious beasts weren't enough to make this a busman's holiday, all does not seem well. "Was it not possible, she asked herself, that she had accidently stumbled upon a mystery?"[31] Indeed, a case of mistaken identity and the rescue of a kidnapped orphan ensue.

For all her cleverness and skill, her advantages and privileges, Bobbie Ann Mason judges Nancy to be "utterly unspoiled and charming." Mason continues, "She is immaculate and self-possessed. . . . She plays parent to frightened children and victims of misfortune, allaying fears and inspiring rapturous confidence instantly with her soothing reasonable voice. . . . Nancy is mistress of the household, and her power extends beyond the home. She gets instant service from policemen, even in a strange town. . . . At all times, Nancy possesses infinite courage, calm, and modesty. . . . She is knowledgeable about any convenient subject. She always has . . . any information needed on a case."[32] A winning combination by any measure.

Thus equipped, it wouldn't be a stretch to say that Nancy Drew's life would appeal to just about any young girl seeking a role model to guide her through adolescence—whether this girl reader pored over the pages during the Great Depression or today—for "the trappings of the mystery genre-crooks, and clues and gothic settings . . . glamorize the trespass into adulthood."[33] Although the character of Nancy Drew has been altered over time, as the series' publishing rights have passed from publisher to publisher and her ghostwriters have exchanged pens, her essential Drew-ness—those timelessly appealing qualities admired and aspired to—has remained the same.

NOTES

1. Merriam-Webster, online edition, s.v. "dame," https://www.merriam-webster.com/dictionary/dame.
2. Rehak, *Girl Sleuth: Nancy Drew*, 101.
3. Ibid., 103.
4. Ibid.
5. Ibid., 104.
6. Ibid., 105.

7. Ibid.
8. Ibid., 107.
9. Ibid.
10. Originally published as Carolyn Keene [Mildred Wirt Benson], *The Mystery at Lilac Inn* (New York: Grosset and Dunlap, 1930). I draw my quotations from a later edition, published as Carolyn Keene, *The Mystery at Lilac Inn*, facsimile edition (Bedford, MA: Applewood Books, 1994), 1. Any quotations hereafter from this title are from the 1994 facsimile edition.
11. Rehak, *Girl Sleuth: Nancy Drew*, 117.
12. Bobbie Ann Mason, *The Girl Sleuth: On the Trail of Nancy Drew, Judy Bolton, and Cherry Ames* (Athens: University of Georgia Press, 1995), 49–50.
13. Brenda Lange, *Edward Stratemeyer: Creator of the Hardy Boys and Nancy Drew* (Philadelphia: Chelsea House Publishers, 2004), 68.
14. Caprio, *Mystery of Nancy Drew*, 91.
15. Ibid.
16. Originally published as Carolyn Keene, *The Bungalow Mystery* (New York: Grosset & Dunlap, 1930). I draw this quotation from a later edition, published as Carolyn Keene, *The Bungalow Mystery* (Bedford, MA: Applewood Books, 1991), 183. Any quotations hereafter from this title are from the 1991 facsimile edition.
17. Keene, *The Secret of the Old Clock*, 6.
18. Keene, *Mystery at Lilac Inn*, 4, 74.
19. Boesky, "Solving the Crime of Modernity," 189.
20. Rehak, *Girl Sleuth: Nancy Drew*, 115.
21. Boesky, "Solving the Crime of Modernity," 125.
22. Rehak, *Girl Sleuth: Nancy Drew*, 117.
23. Ibid., 117.
24. Ibid., 142.
25. Mason, *The Girl Sleuth*, 56.
26. Rehak, *Girl Sleuth: Nancy Drew*, 168.
27. Mason, *The Girl Sleuth*, 62.

28. Caprio, *Mystery of Nancy Drew*, 37.

29. Mason, *The Girl Sleuth*, 63.

30. Originally published as Carolyn Keene, *The Secret at Shadow Ranch* (New York: Grosset & Dunlap, 1931). This quotation from page 45 of the facsimile edition, published as Carolyn Keene, *The Secret at Shadow Ranch*, facsimile edition (Bedford, MA: Applewood Books, 1991). Hereafter all citations from this title are from the facsimile edition.

31. Ibid., 75.

32. Mason, *The Girl Sleuth*, 50–51.

33. Ibid., 6.

Chapter Four

Editing Nancy

The tone Mildred Wirt was taking in developing the first three manuscripts had pleased Edward Stratemeyer, and in fact Nancy's just-so mix of relatable and aspirational made best sellers out of the series' first five books, *The Secret of the Old Clock*, *The Hidden Staircase*, *The Bungalow Mystery*, *The Mystery at Lilac Inn*, and *The Secret of Shadow Ranch*. But Edward Stratemeyer would never see its success.

Early on in the project's development, he had been forced to withdraw from active oversight upon falling seriously ill with pneumonia in the winter of early 1930. He returned to his office greatly weakened the following March, only to fall ill once again. On May 10, 1930, Edward Stratemeyer died, mere days after the publication of *The Secret of the Old Clock*. He died with no male heir, but the syndicate was to be retained as a family concern. So his daughter, Harriet Stratemeyer Adams, scrambled to learn everything she could about her father's business, while Stratemeyer's longtime assistant, Harriet Otis Smith, kept the publishing syndicate going in the immediate aftermath.

It is at this point that the series was increasingly drawn according to Harried Stratemeyer Adams's views. And this was not always consonant with Mildred's vision for Nancy. As far back as the development of *The Mystery at Lilac Inn*, Mildred recalled that "the syndicate's new owner asked that I make the sleuth less bold and that abrupt sentence endings be avoided. In editing, a simple, 'Nancy said' became 'Nancy said sweetly,' 'she said kindly,' and the like, all designed to produce a less abrasive, more caring type of character."[1]

Over the series' long run Nancy would undergo innumerable changes: She would age from sixteen to eighteen. Her sense of fashion always changed to reflect the modes of the day in which each title was published (the cloche hats, drop-waist dresses, and heels of the1930s were spirited away; the Nancy of the 1940s favored victory rolls and sweater sets like any fashionable bobby-soxer). But these changes to Nancy's character—changes influenced by Harriet, and no doubt changing societal mores—were more fundamental.

It was Harriet's idea to give Nancy a boyfriend, which Mildred dutifully wrote into the seventh Nancy Drew Mystery, *The Clue in the Diary*. By the early 1940s, according to Rehak, Nancy Drew's fans began writing the publisher, asking about the status of Nancy and Ned's romantic relationship. Harriet asked Mildred to make Nancy's interest in Ned more obvious—more feminized. Mildred resisted, insisting that romantic portrayals were not her strong suit. However, Harriet's ideas prevailed in *The Secret in the Old Attic*, where Nancy "spends a considerable amount of time hoping [Ned] will invite her to the 'big dance' at Emerson College, showing some uncharacteristic signs of insecurity in the process. 'Maybe Ned has another girl. . . . He has a perfect right to, of course.'"[2]

Nancy's rival for Ned's affections, Diane Dight, attempts to usurp Nancy's place as Ned's date instead. But while in the attic with Ned, solving the attic's "secret," Nancy sees a spider and faints into Ned's arms. And thus "mystery and romance were duly resolved."[3] Shortly thereafter, "alive and well, and in love, the handsome pair dances the night away at Emerson, locked in chaste happiness."[4]

As flawed as her relationship with Ned Nickerson might seem, Nancy's relationship with Carson Drew might have served as a model for a healthy, if idealized, father-daughter relationship.[5] Perhaps Nancy Drew's relationship with her father was drawn specifically in contrast to Edward Stratemeyer's relationship with his own children. Once, when Harriet was asked if she was close to her father, she replied, "No, not that close. . . . I had a very strict father, and also my father never had any mysteries for me to solve."[6]

Whatever the case, over time, as Harriet's interest in the Nancy Drew books grew, the father-daughter relationship fundamentally changed: self-reliance was out, and overprotective parenting was in. Whereas in the series' earlier books Carson Drew had proudly mentored Nancy's career, in these later books he assumed a more authoritarian role, and this new Nancy acquiesced with docility.[7] The very center of Nancy's Drew-ness, it seemed, was in danger of being written out of the series altogether.

Since the onset of World War II, in addition to writing as Carolyn Keene, Mildred Wirt had begun working at the *Toledo Times*, doing what many women did during that time—stepping in to fill the void created when the men had left for the front. And Nancy Drew continued to reflect the independent, can-do spirit of American society prevalent during wartime. When Mildred's husband became seriously ill, and subsequently died in 1947, she needed both jobs to support her family. However, following the end of the war, Harriet and Mildred's discordant views of Nancy became actual disagreement.

Postwar cultural shifts were seeing women back at home again, vacating their jobs to returning soldiers, and, subsequently, home and homemaking were emphasized. It was in this climate that Harriet began to view Nancy as less of an independent character and more of an obedient daughter who did as her father asked. Perhaps because Mildred herself had been worn down in caring for her invalid husband for so long, or perhaps in some calculated reaction to Harriet's criticism, the next Nancy Drew mystery Mildred submitted, *The Mystery of the Tolling Bell*, greatly displeased Harriet. In critiquing the manuscript, Harriet wrote Mildred that "Nancy does not seem like the . . . untiring person she has always been. . . . Nancy spoke in a very adult fashion, and it made her seem much older than in former books."[8]

Eventually Harriet decided to more absolutely direct Nancy's development. In the early 1950s, under the influence of the syndicate's longtime publisher, Grossett & Dunlap, Harriet began to see the advantage of having syndicate staff develop all manuscripts in-house, where she could supervise their progress herself. This made talented freelance authors like Mildred Wirt redundant. Harriet decided to write Nancy herself, assuming the Carolyn Keene pen name. So it was that the thirtieth installment in the Nancy Drew series, *The Clue of the Velvet Mask* (1953), was Mildred Wirt's last as Carolyn Keene.

With Mildred's departure from the Stratemeyer Syndicate, a series of ghostwriters began penning the series titles, and under Harriet Stratemeyer Adams's watchful eye, they systematically softened Nancy's image. Throughout the 1930s and '40s readers had enjoyed the girl sleuth's plucky, independent spirit. But this new Nancy grew less independent than she had been in the first titles, playing the obedient daughter, ever ready to do her father's bidding.

Why the change? Perhaps this new Nancy better reflected the values of post–World War II America, where women were encouraged to return to the hearth and cede their hard-won jobs to returning soldiers. This iteration of Nancy certainly dovetails nicely with the perfect, prim, and pliable domestics modeled in June Cleaver, Donna Reed, and the many other "perfect" women portrayed in the popular TV shows of the era. According to Betsy Caprio, the publisher had believed the original Nancy to be "too bold and bossy" and intentionally set out to soften her image by "send[ing] her to church regularly and generally dispel[ling] Nancy's larger-than-life mystique. Carson Drew, who early in Nancy's career provided his daughter with a revolver, now became a protective dad who forbids her to go sleuthing alone—and most of the time, Nancy obeys him."[9]

And just as Nancy 2.0 grew more compliant and less adventuresome—less recognizably a dame—ironically her circumstances became less relatable to her readers. She increasingly left her hometown and began solving mysteries in big cities and comparatively exotic locales: New Orleans (*The Haunted Showboat*, 1957), San Francisco (*The Mystery of the Fire Dragon*, 1961)—even Scotland (*The Clue of the Whistling Bagpipes*, 1964).

These changes in aggregate negatively alter Nancy's accessibility as a role model. Her agency is diminished—her willingness to say no, her balance of the personal and the public. And none but the very wealthiest of her readers could possibly identify with the ease with which she crosses borders. While it's undeniable that premakeover Nancy enjoyed a level of comfort unavailable to many of her young readers, her high personal standards were always both aspirational *and* attainable, and her achievements were accomplished for the most part on her own turf. Consider most any adolescent reader, who will agonize far more frequently over how to handle the politics of the dinner table, classroom, and playground than anything further from home. As readers grow and work out for themselves the best ways to navigate a complex, contradictory world, this modified Nancy can no longer show them the way, and so they eventually leave her behind.

From irrepressible adventure-seeker to moderated good-girl jet-setter, Nancy's alteration reflects the mores and worldviews of the multiple pens bringing her to life and the changing times in which her stories were written. The cultural shifts resulting from the civil rights and women's liberation movements of the 1960s and '70s recast Nancy, too, though not in as straightforward a fashion as one might think. While American culture at large grappled with what it meant to bring once-taboo topics into the public sphere, scholars of race relations trained a magnifying glass on old prejudices and feminists sought to integrate sexuality into an understanding of modern womanhood. But change comes in fits and starts, and the zigzagging path taken by Nancy's character exemplified how confusing the discussion can be.

For all her competencies—for all that was admirable and good about Nancy Drew—she still took on many of the prejudices and ignorance of her time. Specifically, she reflected a white-privileged classism that was especially underscored in her interactions with African Americans, immigrants, and people living outside of upper-middle-class River Heights. "Negroes," as Carolyn Keene called them—the term *African American* not yet in use—first appeared in Nancy's stratified world in the series' very first volume.

And after four decades of publication, academia began to call into public question some of the series' most discordant prejudices. In a 1971 article published in *The Journal of Negro Education*, James P. Jones calls out the racial stereotypes appearing in the first Nancy Drew mysteries alone. Of the few Negroes written into the series at all, "most," Jones writes, "are faceless menials of no significance to the development of the stories. . . . The seventeen Negroes include five maids, four porters, two cooks, one caretaker, one butler, one elevator 'starter,' one woman who applies for work as a servant, and two men with no occupation other than their criminal activities."[10] What few African American characters there were, were presented unfavorably.

Carolyn Keene, Jones points out, refers to these characters as "colored women" or "colored porters" and further identifies them by their ungrammatical language: "Double negatives, slang, or dropped endings abound."[11] Further, Jones states, "the roles assigned Negroes by Carolyn Keene surely served to reinforce an unfair, distorted, and harmful stereotype,"[12] as "Nancy Drew's readers were . . . faced with evidence that Negroes lied, drank to excess, had a tendency toward crime, and often behaved irresponsibly on their jobs."[13]

In *The Mystery at Lilac Inn*, when the Drews' longtime housekeeper, Hannah Gruen, has to leave town, Nancy conducts a series of interviews to find a temporary replacement. When a "colored woman" arrives at the Drew home for an interview, Nancy opens the door, and "her heart sank within her. It was indeed the colored woman sent by the employment agency, but a more unlikely housekeeper Nancy had ever seen. She was dirty and slovenly and had an unpleasant way of shuffling her feet when she walked."[14]

Nancy then laments to her father what difficulty she had identifying appropriate help, "emit[ing] a tired sigh as she unfastened her apron. 'This morning the agency sent me an Irish woman, but she was even worse than the one that came yesterday. She was the most unreasonable housekeeper I ever interviewed.'"[15] Nancy inevitably hires Mrs. Sadie Carter, "an elderly woman who suited her in every way."[16] The reader can assume Mrs. Carter was white.

These unflattering, damaging characterizations of most anyone who wasn't white and upper-middle-class stood in the series for decades. Finally, amid the racial upheaval of the fight for civil rights in the 1960s, Grosset & Dunlap subsequently agreed it was time to update the books, excising some of the most offensive language.

But not all updates to Nancy were as kind. In 1986, Simon & Schuster, the series' new publisher, rebooted the series as *The Nancy Drew Files*. This updated Nancy was redrawn as a glamorous, globe-trotting professional private investigator who solved murders for hire—now with 90 percent more sex appeal! Picture Nancy in a bikini, cavorting on a Bahaman beach with Ned Nickerson. This drastic makeover hadn't been Nancy's first eye-raising sexualization; the star of the short-lived 1970s TV show *The Nancy Drew Mysteries* had posed for *Playboy* during the show's run.

But while the brand's managers may have been responding to an increasingly sexualized culture, they'd overstepped: This glamazon, sex-pot Nancy Drew was not well-received. The publishers quickly came to their senses and brought back the plucky, down-to-earth Nancy of old, this time electing for more moderate updates: This latest Nancy uses more slang and has been known to slip her credit card from her purse to unlock a door, and the famous blue roadster has been upgraded to a blue Mustang. And the books were printed only in paperback. But trade out the acid-washed jeans for a drop-waist skirt, and readers will recognize in this late-twentieth-century model a reasonable facsimile of the original Nancy.

The publishers made sure to leaven any updates with welcome throwbacks to the mysteries' earliest days. After a long hiatus, Nancy's ever-loyal chums Bess and George were reintroduced to the series, and Ned was downgraded from panting lover back to charming escort. Carson Drew once again mellowed into the indulgent father who takes his daughter seriously and regards her as a professional peer. Housekeeper Hannah Gruen once again polished the Drew household to a shine. And Nancy was back in her element: River Heights was just as fraught with solvable crime as ever.

Nancy's character having come full circle, her most-treasured traits restored, we once again remember why we hold the original Nancy Drew up as a role model for today's girls. Present-day Nancy may be plucky once again, her essential Drew-ness renewed, and yet it is still the Nancy of the 1930s who can most powerfully speak to young girls of the twenty-first century. The original mysteries by Mildred Wirt seem timeless in part because current events never enter the plot. And although Nancy's mannerisms are typical of the period, and though she meets any of the gender expectations of the day, she is simultaneously, ever graciously, embodying more typically male traits. She embodies the best of female and male expectation with grace. And it is Nancy's effortless straddling of the feminine and male spheres that I consider worthy role modeling for today's young women. This is the essence of Nancy's Drew-ness: intelligence, loyalty, kindness, independence, poise, and gumption.

Nancy Drew of the early twentieth century is a poster girl for the new millennium.

NOTES

1. From Mildred Benson's introduction to Keene, *Mystery at Lilac Inn*, 7.
2. Rehak, *Girl Sleuth: Nancy Drew*, 206.
3. Ibid.
4. Ibid., 207.
5. Caprio, *Mystery of Nancy Drew*, 93.
6. As quoted in ibid., 92.
7. Caprio, *Mystery of Nancy Drew*, 22.
8. Rehak, *Girl Sleuth: Nancy Drew*, 220.
9. Caprio, *Mystery of Nancy Drew*, 22.
10. James P. Jones, "Negro Stereotypes in Children's Literature: The Case of Nancy Drew," *The Journal of Negro Education* 40, no. 2 (Spring 1971): 122.
11. Ibid.
12. Ibid., 125.
13. Ibid., 123.
14. Keene, *Mystery at Lilac Inn*, 16.
15. Ibid., 17.
16. Ibid., 25.

Chapter Five

Drew-ness in the Twenty-First Century

Nancy Drew, assuming she's a fan of good TV, might recognize herself in a few of the most compelling representations of female empowerment in the twenty-first century. When *Veronica Mars* creator Rob Thomas first introduced his "teen noir" to audiences in 2004, Veronica joined Buffy the Vampire Slayer and Jessica Jones in a sisterhood of female heroines whose compelling mix of virtues and vices, light and dark, masculine and feminine, would provide a twenty-first-century update to their prototype, Nancy Drew. Integral to what makes these strong female characters so appealing today is their mix of sugar and spice—maybe a little heavier on the spice.

Blonde and attractive, Veronica Mars seems to live a charmed life in her fictional Southern Californian town of Neptune: she's popular, easily earns good grades, and has a handsome, athletic boyfriend. Remind you of anyone? But while Nancy lives in ease and successfully concludes every caper, for decades in succession, Veronica's fortune is evidently too good to last for modern television viewers.

When *Veronica Mars* first opens, her world has just been upended with the murder of her best friend—and boyfriend's sister—Lily Kane. Veronica's father, Keith Mars, is Neptune's sheriff, and after initial investigation points to the powerful, wealthy Kane family itself, Keith arrests Lily's father for the murder. But this proves a politically unpopular move in a town whose industry is based on the highly successful Kane Software company. After a recall election, Sheriff Mars loses his job in disgrace, his wife leaves, and, overnight, Veronica becomes a pariah at Neptune High. Down but not out, Keith Mars uses everything he has learned in law enforcement to open a detective agency, where Veronica helps out in a secretarial capacity after school. The business is struggling, and Veronica, left adrift her raft of personal tragedies, struggles, too. Even so, she never wavers in a single-minded determination to solve the murder of her best friend.

Throughout the show's first season, viewers see Veronica train her keen intelligence, technical savvy, and pure moxie on chipping away at the mysteries obscuring the Lily Kane murder. And Veronica's not above purposing her significant personal abilities to target her nemeses—Neptune High's popular clique, the very friends who deserted her when her fortunes turned. Learning from her father's example, Veronica picks herself back up again and parlays her pariah status into a business opportunity, making money on the side as an investigator-for-hire among her new social stratum, Neptune's motley outcasts.

A sharp cultural demarcation divides the haves and have-nots in Veronica's town. At Neptune High, the wealthy kids are referred to as the "09ers," a reference to their tony zip code, 90909. Compare this to the PCHers, Neptune's resident biker gang, named for the strip of the Pacific Coast Highway they territorialize. And where the 09ers all drive luxury cars—the latest BMW and Mercedes models—other students have to take the bus to school, emphasizing their orbit far outside the 09er epicenter of cool. Veronica, however, is saved from that particular indignity, as she has her own car—a Chrysler LeBaron convertible, nowhere near as cool as Nancy's trick blue roadster.

As the series opens, in a bitter voiceover Veronica quickly brings us up to speed: how her formerly enchanted life has been shattered by Lily's murder; how her father has lost elected office after arresting the most popular, and arguably powerful, man in all of Neptune; how her mother, unable to take the strain of the family's reduced circumstances, has abandoned them; how her boyfriend has unceremoniously dumped her after the shock of his sister's murder and his father's arrest; how this means she has lost her 09er cred, and all of her social circle along with it. Then Veronica tells us how right after her social takedown she defiantly crashes an 09er party, where she consumes a drink that, unbeknownst to her, has been drugged. Consequently, she passes out. When she wakes the following morning, she realizes she has been raped while unconscious. Dazed she goes to the authorities to report the crime, but the new sheriff refuses to take her seriously—and even cruelly takes the opportunity to mock the daughter of his deposed, former boss. It is this culmination of events that, according to critics Tamy Burnett and Melissa Townsend, "irrevocably alter[s] Veronica's view of justice and her own safety in her world; because of this shift, *Veronica Mars* begins with its heroine a sarcastic, cynical young women whose penchant for vengeance is easily understood."[1]

The trauma permeates Veronica, and her very appearance changes in response: from hyper-feminine SoCal glam—long, bright blonde hair; short-skirted dresses in pastels—to a more androgynous, goth-light look—jeans, T-shirts, Doc Martens, and leather jackets. She has made a conscious decision to recast her identity and embrace her exclusion (if treated like an outcast, why not dress the part?). When asked by a fellow student how she copes with the serial mistreatment by her peers, Veronica offers her guiding philosophy: "Here's what you do: You get tough. You get even."[2]

With the complete rejection of her previous persona, and compelled to discover the truth behind Lily's murder, gnarled and knotted and uncomfortable though her discoveries may prove to be, Veronica assumes certain Sam Spade–ish traits often found in the traditional noir film; "the dry, ironic voiceovers," for example, "which begin most episodes,"[3] are a way "to describe storytelling with a dark edge."[4] It is also characteristic of noir films for the detective—or, in this case, Veronica—to "not let danger stop her search for the truth."[5] But she's no fool tempting fate; modern girl that she is, Veronica carries a Taser as backup—just in case.

The first season of the show is propelled by Veronica's search for Lily's murderer and for her own rapist. And any opportunity Veronica finds to exact revenge on her former, turncoat, friends is a good opportunity, however petty. Adding to her misery, though Veronica is a very bright and a gifted student—she takes all AP courses in school—she always seems to end up a target of school authorities looking to blame someone for whatever fresh mischief befalls Neptune High. Whether it's contraband found in a locker or computer passwords compromised, somehow the finger is always pointed at Veronica. In the pilot episode, the principal wearily asks her, "Why does trouble follow you around?"[6]

But, though we meet Veronica in a very dark place, she is not completely disillusioned. Amid her own search for murderers and quest for vengeance, she continues to be guided by a higher sense of justice. She has empathy for her "uncool" classmates, particularly now that she is one of them. She often comes to their aid—however resentfully at first—particularly when they have fallen victim to an injustice, and in the end she always manages to help them out. In fact, it's Veronica's grudging chivalry that, quite unintentionally, wins her a new—and solitary—friend: She alone in a group of gawking students comes to the aid of a new student, Wallace Fennel, who has been targeted for harassment by the PCHers. After Veronica suspiciously circles Wallace over the course of the pilot episode, the two fall into a warm, stabilizing, mutually beneficial friendship that endures for the series' duration. And it isn't long before Wallace, always privy to the details of Veronica's latest case, becomes her "sidekick in crime."

As her reputation for assisting classmates in trouble grows, she increasingly finds herself cornered in the privacy of her "office"—the girls' bathroom across from her locker at Neptune High—beseeched to get to the bottom of some trouble or other. And she always does. One of her pet crusades is avenging young women who, like her, have been sexually importuned in some manner; Veronica is deeply, bitterly aware of the gender inequities in the world.

Veronica is so effective as an unofficial PI not only because of her devastating intellect and a fearlessness born of weary disappointments. Ever-observant, Veronica—like Nancy before her—has long been learning at the knee of her supercompetent father, first in his role as sheriff and now as operator of Mars Investigations. She knows his tricks of the trade and, whenever his back is turned, takes advantage of his access to any number of databases and useful informants. No mere ditzy, helpless Valley Girl, Veronica is astute, driven, and well equipped—and in perfect position to solve Lily Kane's murder, avenge her own assault, and make a little cash with her side hustle.

After she has been ejected from the rarefied 09er atmosphere, Veronica quickly reorients herself, managing to travel her world with agency. It's "because of her exiled status," suggests *Teen Television*, that Veronica "does not adopt class as her defining identity marker and, as a result, demonstrates a great deal of freedom."[7] And in embracing her freedom, Veronica grows unafraid to speak truth to power. She locates advantage in her very marginalization: she has nothing to lose.

One need not dig deep to identify numerous parallels between Veronica Mars and her antecedent, Nancy Drew. Both amateur detectives know popularity, good looks, intelligence, and curiosity. They are also athletic, resourceful, and independent. They have been raised in single-parent homes—their mothers having been written out of the picture before we even get to know them—by doting, keenly intelligent fathers who work in the legal arena.

We've already seen how Nancy Drew's life might appeal to any young girl reader of the Depression era seeking a role model while navigating adolescence. But Nancy's best traits are timeless, and her fans of today would find her just as unerring a guide, for "the trappings of the mystery genre—crooks and clues and gothic settings . . . glamorize the trespass into adulthood."[8] However, for all of Nancy Drew's prowess in solving thorny mysteries, for all the physical prowess she puts to good use when escaping some nefarious villain or other, she embodies a traditional femininity in her demeanor as well as in her apparel. In as much agency as she possesses, she also operates well within the acceptable norms of the traditional heterosexual female. Compare this exemplar of early twentieth-century girlhood to the jaded, world-weary, caustic Veronica we meet in episode 1; even by modern standards

Veronica's edge is cutting. And the way these two girl sleuths fare and move in the world differs, too: in River Heights, Nancy enjoys the privileges, trust, and comforts accorded to being the daughter of the powerful, successful Carson Drew, whereas Neptune more or less regards Veronica with distrust, disrespect, and resentment.

But differ in style as they do, both characters are admired for their ability to operate as independent actors in their worlds. Both enjoy close relationships with their fathers and assist them in their respective businesses. Both are raised without mothers—though it behooves us to underscore that Nancy's mother has died, whereas Veronica has been abandoned by her mother, who later briefly reenters the picture only long enough to kindle Veronica's hopes of a reunion and happy ending. Lianne Mars is a drunk, and when she once again absconds, first draining Veronica's college fund to pay for her habit, Veronica is devastated and cuts her mother out of her life altogether. Not all single parenthoods are created equal.

And so Veronica's aggressive refusal to be anyone's victim, to remain quiet and cowed in the corner, is a neat mirror to the agency and ease that has maintained Nancy Drew's popularity since the 1930s—albeit as a person of privilege navigating a heteronormative and homogenous universe. In River Heights, there are clear demarcations between social classes: the criminals live in a specific part of the town and are portrayed as being of lower economic status than Nancy and her cohort. And while Veronica informs us that Neptune is a town with "no middle class"[9]—bisecting the social classes neatly into the rich and the not-rich—River Heights is divided into more disparate castes: the upper-middle class, such as the Drews; the non–WASP criminal element living on the wrong side of town; and the servant class, consisting of the "help," such as Hannah

Gruen, who so ably manages the Drew household and, in Mrs. Drew's absence, stands in as the series' figure of domesticity. In Nancy's world, even as trouble lurks, it is always solvable, and by the final page the world has settled neatly back into its proscribed order.

Nancy Drew's manner is consistently ladylike, and when she does get into trouble, she always finds a way out; no Taser, or any other weapon, is necessary. In fact, the Stratemeyer Publishing Syndicate specifically prohibited Nancy from having anything to do with guns and subsequent violence. Aside from the time Nancy carried the pistol at the ranch, the series broke the ban only one other time, early on in publication, when Carson Drew gives Nancy a small revolver to carry in her purse; but she never uses it. In other words, in Nancy Drew's world, the trouble may be bad, but it never rises to the level of human bloodshed. And even when things get sticky, her chums are always there to lend moral support. But Bess and George seldom directly assist Nancy, unlike Wallace, who jumps into the melee—sometimes an actual melee—whenever Veronica needs a hand.

But though Nancy was written onto the advantaged side of sharply drawn class lines, and though the peril she faces never results in violence, she is anything but weak, passive, or idle. While we often see her come to the aid of those in her own social class who have been victimized—their heirloom jewels have been stolen, or a will has gone missing, or the *heir* to that will has gone missing—Nancy often goes out of her way to assist those in less comfortable circumstances than hers. In *The Secret of Red Gate Farm*, Nancy helps two sisters living in poor, rural isolation regain their rightful inheritance. And while Nancy's accomplishments are outsized, she is ever modest about them, always refusing any monetary reward for her successes, although she has been known to accept a piece of jewelry every now and then by way of thanks. Veronica Mars is somewhat more hard-boiled in that regard; she often charges a fee for her services, ostensibly putting her earnings away for college. But to be fair, the Mars family has fallen on hard financial times, whereas the Drew household is prosperous and stable. And for all her capitalist streak, Veronica often betrays a soft spot when it comes to fighting injustices or preventing the powerful from preying on the vulnerable; nothing but danger and retaliation could have awaited her after she took revenge on the motorcycle gang bullying her friend Wallace. He understands her best, in all her complexity. "Underneath that 'angry young woman' shell there's a slightly less angry young woman," he reads her. "You're a marshmallow, Veronica Mars—a Twinkie."[10]

This mix of light and dark, soft and hard, tempers the brooding noir element that permeates *Veronica Mars*. But that bleak cynicism is totally absent from the Nancy Drew mysteries—somewhat ironic, given that noir mysteries and, later, films were in full vogue for adults the same time the Stratemeyer Syndicate was first drawing Nancy. Perhaps early twentieth-century readers were not prepared to see such hardness and world-weariness in their heroines. By way of comparison, the *New York Times*'s Alessandra Stanley calls Veronica Mars "an amateur sleuth who is closer in spirit to Philip Marlowe than to Nancy Drew."[11] But perhaps it's more on the mark to think of Veronica Mars as a more daring cousin of Nancy Drew, although critic Terry Kelleher has pointed out that "The Nancy Drew stories do not begin with Nancy staking out a 'hot-sheets' motel and sharing with her audience 'a lurid recollection of the night she lost her virginity.'"[12] I doubt Nancy's sometime-beau Ned Nickerson ever got past a chaste goodnight kiss following the country club dance; contrast this with Veronica necking in a jeep, being swept off her feet into her boyfriend's hotel room, and generally enjoying sex throughout the series. But even if the sensibilities of sixteen-year-olds today might skew slightly more Veronica than Nancy, and Nancy's "ladylike" manners notwithstanding generally, Nancy Drew still stands as a model of female agency, even among a readership whose parents have long since given them the birds-and-the-bees talk.

For all their similarities and dissimilarities, Nancy and Veronica are of a piece—strong, independently minded young women who do not curb their natural curiosity but leverage it to make their world a better place. Now, Nancy's righting of wrongs seems motivated by a sense of morality that is more traditional and class-based, in that from her perch of privilege a kind of noblesse oblige enables her to extend herself to the person in need. Veronica, on the other hand, is on a mission of justice and personal vengeance. Her disillusionment with the world has left her angry and determined to claw back justice wherever she might; it also compels her to seek resolution for her rape. But Veronica's loss of faith and innocence does not leave her broken and weak: she has transformed into the "outspoken avenger of the powerless."[13] Perhaps Nancy Drew's adventures might reassure us that in the end everything will be all right. Veronica Mars tells us that even if it isn't, we are not powerless.

Netflix and Marvel Comics have recently collaborated to present the television series *Jessica Jones*, based on the character by Brian Michael Bendis and Michael Gaydos. The present-day Jessica Jones is a former super heroine and the owner and sole employee of Alias Investigations. She works within the dark urbanity of the city, in contrast to the sunny climes of

Veronica Mars's hometown of Neptune, California, and Nancy Drew's idyllic suburb of Middle American River Heights.

Jessica retains the vestiges of remaining superpower, however. As a child she was in a car accident with a military convoy carrying radioactive chemicals. Her parents were killed, and Jessica remained in a coma. Upon awakening, Jessica discovers that she now has superhuman strength and a limited ability to overcome mind control. This ability becomes crucial to her survival, because her archenemy possesses the power of mind control over his mostly female victims. Kilgrave, as he styles himself, delights in preying on women, getting them to do anything he wants, smiling, even against their will. Under his cruel puppetry, they suffer unimaginable humiliation, including sexual abuse.

Unfortunately for Jessica, she catches Kilgrave's eye one night while she is stopping a mugging. Kilgrave grows instantly obsessed with her and kidnaps her. At this point, she does not yet know how to marshal all of her superpowers, and her limited ability to overcome mind control is no match for Kilgrave. He tortures her for one year, psychologically as well as physically, and it is only after Jessica murders a woman under Kilgrave's orders that she manage to break his mental hold and escape his clutches.

In the aftermath of her abduction and torture, Jessica suffers from post-traumatic stress disorder. She is wracked with guilt that she was unable to escape for so long and that her heightened powers means Kilgrave had in her a lethal weapon. Her guilt over the death of the woman she killed consumes her. She descends into darkness and self-loathing.

To get by, she uses her keen mind and supernormal abilities to run a successful if shoestring detective agency. And in coming to the aid of the oppressed, she seeks to right the scales of justice that she had unwillingly helped unbalance so precariously.

Like Veronica Mars, Jessica Jones seeks to avenge those who have wronged her. Like Veronica, she has been traumatized by sexual abuse. But unlike Veronica, who takes refuge in maintaining excellent grades in her AP classes at Neptune High while assisting classmates in righting the wrongs done against them, Jessica has difficulty functioning. Writer Laura Durkay characterizes Jessica as "traumatized, angry, fearful, guilt-ridden, self-isolating, and probably an alcoholic—barely holding together a life as an underemployed freelancer, working at night or getting blackout drunk because she is afraid to go to sleep."[14]

Both heroines adapted an androgynous "uniform" of leather jacket, T-shirt, jeans, and heavy, dark footwear following their respective sexual assaults. Jessica "considers her clothing to be an armor and a shield and something that helps her maintain a distance from other people," says *Jessica Jones* fashion designer Stephanie Maslansky. "It keeps her from having to deal with the rest of humanity."[15] For both of these traumatized women, this style of dress also serves to deflect the male gaze—especially important in Jessica's case, where "Kilgrave's power is the literal embodiment of extreme male entitlement."[16]

Both *Veronica Mars* and *Jessica Jones* allegorize female vengeance; although Veronica Mars solves injustices mostly within the realm of adolescence, she does so within the context of adult corruption, rape, and murder. Jessica Jones deals more directly with urban violence and her own dysfunction. In contrast, Nancy Drew, always "ladylike" in her manner and dress, deals with the comparatively benign crimes of theft and, like Veronica and Jessica, functions in the adult realm. Yet she also seeks to right wrongs and therefore dwells within a similar moral universe as do Veronica and Jessica, albeit a universe much less fraught with overt sexual violence. I refer to Nancy's Drew-ness—that which has remained consistent over the years in the character: her ability to maintain agency and adhere to a moral compass regardless of the circumstances. This is something the three characters share.

And so in TV reruns Veronica Mars continues to assist her father at his detective agency, follow the clues to figure out who raped her and who murdered her best friend, and alleviate the suffering of anyone sentenced to take the bus to school. As of this writing, season 2 of *Jessica Jones*, just released, promises to show our troubled heroine cope with life as best she can in the dark urban jungle, looking out for signs of Kilgrave, and ever on the alert for those who have been wronged.

The bruised and brooding Veronica and Jessica seem to speak to a once-bitten section of today's female viewership. So where does the bright and personable Nancy fit in with her twenty-first-century sisters? The differences in tone and scope are drastic. River Heights's most celebrated citizen, ever chipper, is never personally afflicted, existing above the fray, and managing to never sully herself as she scolds the unsavory back into good behavior. The idea of Nancy as a victim of bullying or kidnapping or sex crime is unthinkable. So why consider Nancy Drew a relevant role model for today's young girls? The original Nancy, the Nancy whom Mildred Wirt first brought to life in the 1930s, is allowed to exist out of time, because contemporary news events never find their way into her pages while at the same time her virtues are modern. True, Nancy's manners are typical of a well-behaving girl of the 1930s, and her milieu and aspirations are representative of her gender sphere. But early Nancy blurs the edges between gender spheres, graciously—laughingly, nonthreateningly—embodying traits accorded well-behaving *boys* of the 1930s. But it's not only a Depression-era reader who is well-served by a heroine whose feet are firmly planted on the ground but whose fearlessness in moving through the world and accepting her best traits are aspirational. Veronica Mars and Jessica Jones function as an iteration of Nancy burdened by twenty-first-century problems; their viewers recognize the poverty, violence, and misogyny that assault them. But their viewers also see that when the chips are down these women double down on their strength, intelligence, curiosity, problem-solving, and empathy to nudge the world a little closer toward justice.

So whether it's looking to Nancy, to Veronica, or to Jessica, today's young women can find worthy role models in any woman who embodies that excellent blend of masculine and feminine traits—that Drew-ness: intelligence, loyalty, kindness, independence, poise, and, especially, "moxie and a good sense of balance . . . when crawling on a roof."[17] For "there are fighting days still ahead of all of us," points out author Melanie Rehak, and we'll be looking to Nancy and her ilk to show us the way.[18]

NOTES

1. Tamy Burnett and Melissa Townsend, "Rethinking 'The Getting Even' Part: Feminist Anger and Vigilante Justice in a Post–9/11 America," in *Investigating "Veronica Mars": Essays on the Teen Detective Series*, ed. Rhonda V. Wilcox and Sue Turnbull (Jefferson, NC: McFarland, 2011), 96.

2. Veronica in episode 1.8, quoted in ibid., 95.

3. Rhonda V. Wilcox and Sue Turnbull, "Introduction: Canonical Veronica; *Veronica Mars* and Vintage Television," in *Investigating "Veronica Mars": Essays on the Teen Detective Series*, ed. Rhonda V. Wilcox and Sue Turnbull (Jefferson, NC: McFarland, 2011), 6.

4. Author and literary critic Lani Diane Rich, as quoted in Burnett and Townsend, "Rethinking 'The Getting Even Part,'" 99.

5. Wilcox and Turnbull, "Introduction: Canonical Veronica," 6.

6. Kristen Bell, Percy Daggs III, Teddy Dunn, and Rob Thomas, season 1, episode 1, "Pilot," *Veronica Mars: The Complete First Season* (Burbank, CA: Warner Home Video, 2004), DVD.

7. Quoted in Sharon Marie Ross and Louisa Ellen Stein, eds., *Teen Television: Essays on Programming and Fandom* (Jefferson, NC: McFarland, 2008), 108.

8. Mason, *The Girl Sleuth*, 6.

9. Rob Thomas, ed., *Neptune Noir: Unauthorized Investigations into Veronica Mars*, with Leah Wilson (Dallas: BenBella Books, 2006), 83.

10. Bell, Daggs III, Dunn, and Thomas, season 1, episode 1, "Pilot."

11. Alessandra Stanley, "A Junior Detective at Hard-Boiled High," *New York Times*, September 20, 2004, http://www.nytimes.com/2004/09/20/arts/television/a-junior-detective-at-hardboiled-high.html.

12. Kelleher quoted in Tanya R. Cochran, "Neptune (Non-)Consensual: The Risky Business of Television Fandom, Falling in Love, and Playing the Victim," in *Investigating "Veronica Mars": Essays on the Teen Detective Series*, ed. Rhonda V. Wilcox and Sue Turnbull (Jefferson, NC: McFarland, 2011), 175.

13. Sarah Whitney, "'No Longer That Girl': Rape Narrative and Meaning in *Veronica Mars*," in *Investigating "Veronica Mars": Essays on the Teen Detective Series*, ed. Rhonda V. Wilcox and Sue Turnbull (Jefferson, NC: McFarland, 2011), 154.

14. Laura Durkay, "Jessica Jones' Superpower Is Surviving," *Green Left Weekly*, no. 1083, February 9, 2016, https://www.greenleft.org.au/content/jessica-jones-superpower-surviving.

15. Fawnia Soo Hoo, "There Are No Super Hero Costumes to Be Found in 'Jessica Jones,' Netflix's Latest Marvel Adaptation," *Fashionista*, November 20, 2015 https://fashionista.com/2015/11/jessica-jones-costume.

16. Durkay, "Jessica Jones' Superpower Is Surviving."

17. Worick, *Nancy Drew's Guide to Life*, 12.

18. Rehak, *Girl Sleuth: Nancy Drew*, 314.

Bibliography

Bell, Kristen, Percy Daggs, III, Teddy Dunn, and Rob Thomas. Blurb from DVD case. *Veronica Mars: The Complete First Season*. Burbank, CA: Warner Home Video, 2004. DVD.

Billman, Carol. *The Secret of the Stratemeyer Syndicate: Nancy Drew, the Hardy Boys, and the Million Dollar Fiction Factory*. New York: The Ungar Publishing Company, 1986.

Boesky, Amy. "Solving the Crime of Modernity: Nancy Drew in 1930." Studies in the Novel. *The Young Adult Novel* 42, nos. 1–2 (Spring and Summer 2010): 185–201.

Burnett, Tamy, and Melissa Townsend. "Rethinking 'The Getting Even Part': Feminist Anger and Vigilante Justice in a Post–9/11 America." In *Investigating "Veronica Mars": Essays on the Teen Detective Series*, edited by Rhonda V. Wilcox and Sue Turnbull, 95–109. Jefferson, NC: McFarland, 2011.

Caprio, Betsy. *The Mystery of Nancy Drew: Girl Sleuth on the Couch*. Trabuco Canyon, CA: Source Books, 1992.

Cochran, Tanya R. "Neptune (Non-)Consensual: The Risky Business of Television Fandom, Falling in Love, and Playing the Victim." In *Investigating "Veronica Mars": Essays on the Teen Detective Series*, edited by Rhonda V. Wilcox and Sue Turnbull, 167–188. Jefferson, NC: McFarland, 2011.

Durkay, Laura. "Jessica Jones' Superpower Is Surviving." *Green Left Weekly*, no. 1083, February 9, 2016. https://www.greenleft.org.au/content/jessica-jones-superpower-surviving.

Harrison, Jessica. "Girl Sleuth: Timeless Nancy Drew Series Celebrates 80 Years of Popularity." *Deseret News*, May 17, 2010. https://www.deseretnews.com/article/700032881/Girl-sleuth-Timeless-Nancy-Drew-series-celebrates-80-years-of-popularity.html.

Jones, James P. "Negro Stereotypes in Children's Literature: The Case of Nancy Drew." *The Journal of Negro Education* 40, no. 2 (Spring 1971): 121–25.

Keene, Carolyn [Mildred Wirt Benson]. *The Bungalow Mystery*. New York: Grosset & Dunlap, 1931.

———. *The Bungalow Mystery*. Facsimile edition. Bedford, MA: Applewood Books, 1991.

———. *The Mystery at Lilac Inn*. New York: Grosset & Dunlap, 1930.

———. *The Mystery at Lilac Inn*, facsimile edition. Bedford, MA: Applewood Books, 1994.

———. *The Secret at Shadow Ranch*. New York: Grosset & Dunlap, 1931.

———. *The Secret at Shadow Ranch*. Facsimile edition. Bedford, MA: Applewood Books, 1991.

———. *The Secret of the Old Clock*. New York: Grosset & Dunlop, 1930.

———. *The Secret of the Old Clock*. Facsimile edition. Bedford, MA: Applewood Books, 1991.

Kismaric, Carole, and Marvin Heiferman. *The Mysterious Case of Nancy Drew and the Hardy Boys*. New York: Simon & Schuster, 1998.

Lange, Brenda. *Edward Stratemeyer: Creator of the Hardy Boys and Nancy Drew*. Philadelphia: Chelsea House Publishers, 2004.

Marcus, Leonard S. *Minders of Make-Believe: Idealists, Entrepreneurs, and the Shaping of American Children's Literature*. New York: Houghton Mifflin Co., 2008.

Mason, Bobbie Ann. *The Girl Sleuth: On the Trail of Nancy Drew, Judy Bolton, and Cherry Ames*. Athens: University of Georgia Press, 1995.

Rehak, Melanie. *Girl Sleuth: Nancy Drew and the Women Who Created Her*. Orlando: Harcourt, 2005.

Ross, Sharon Marie, and Louisa Ellen Stein, eds. *Teen Television: Essays on Programming and Fandom*. Jefferson, NC: McFarland, 2008.

Savage, Jon. *Teenage: The Prehistory of Youth Culture, 1875–1945*. New York: Penguin Books, 2007.

Soo Hoo, Fawnia. "There Are No Super Hero Costumes to Be Found in 'Jessica Jones,' Netflix's Latest Marvel Adaptation." *Fashionista*, November 20, 2015. https://fashionista.com/2015/11/jessica-jones-costume.

Sullivan, Mark. *Our Times: The United States, 1900–1925*. Vol. 6, The Twenties. New York: Charles Scribner's Sons, 1935.

Thomas, Rob, ed. *Neptune Noir: Unauthorized Investigations into Veronica Mars*. With Leah Wilson. Dallas: BenBella Books, 2006.

Whitney, Sarah. "'No Longer That Girl': Rape Narrative and Meaning in *Veronica Mars*. In *Investigating "Veronica Mars": Essays on the Teen Detective Series*, edited by Rhonda V. Wilcox and Sue Turnbull, 152–66. Jefferson, NC: McFarland, 2011.

Wilcox, Rhonda V., and Sue Turnbull, eds. *Investigating "Veronica Mars": Essays on the Teen Detective Series*. Jefferson, NC: McFarland, 2011.

Worick, Jennifer. *Nancy Drew's Guide to Life*. Philadelphia: Running Press, 2001.

About the Author

Lynne Byall Benson is lecturer in the department of Women's, Gender, and Sexuality Studies at the University of Massachusetts Boston as well as adjunct professor at Bunker Hill Community College in Boston. She received her master's and doctoral degrees from Cornell University. She resides with her husband, John, and their English springer spaniel, Tucker, in the Charlestown neighborhood of Boston. Dr. Benson has been a fan of Nancy Drew since the age of nine.

CPSIA information can be obtained
at www.ICGtesting.com
Printed in the USA
LVHW110955081122
732644LV00004B/87